≽ε ≽ε ≽ε *Walking Out*

❧ ❧ ❧ *Walking Out*

Poems by BETTY ADCOCK

LOUISIANA STATE UNIVERSITY PRESS

BATON ROUGE

1975

For Don and Sylvia, light that stays

PS
3551
D396
W3

Some of the poems in this volume have previously
appeared in the following publications, to which grateful
acknowledgment is made: *Cafe Solo, Carolina Quarter-
ly, Chicago Review, Crazy Horse, Greensboro Review,
Hyperion, Mississippi Review, Nation, New American
Review, New Salt Creek Reader, Pebble, Poetry
Northwest, Southern Poetry Review, Tennessee Poetry
Journal.*
"Water" originally appeared in *I Have Been Hungry
All The Years,* published by Solo Press.
"Ripe" originally appeared in *Chicago Review,*
Vol. 25, No. 4, p. 138; copyright 1974 by *Chicago Review.*

ISBN 0–8071–0154–0
Library of Congress Catalog Card Number   74–82000

Contents

I

❧ ❧ ❧ *After Love*

Identity

"... a woman *is* her mother,
that's the main thing."

ANNE SEXTON

There was a yellow dress with dots,
white shoes with straps.
In a snapshot, black hair merged with shadow
holding the sick face clear.
I could think I never heard her voice.
And that is all
except that I played the last day out
where people were distracted, quiet.
I remember that
and her name frozen in a stone.
I watered it
from vases full of early blooms.

Aunts and cousins bent to kiss
stayed on for years and years
They drew me up
tight-lipped on my only stalk.

Grown now into my life, I own it
like any house freezing to permanence
the dust love makes.
All day I tap messages as though no one could hear,
my voice flaking the way stone flakes
in underbrush and weather.
Cold at the clenched heart's center,
the self fails again,
that stranger.

3

Ripe

Even after I had grown
a household, I could spend
hours belly-down in grass,
watching.

Stillness was all
but for the ant's twitch,
the spider's hair of sound,
the grasshopper's one spur.

Now a motion has overtaken me,
the turning that happens
at the center of stones.

It is not what I was leaning after.
The kite in the wind comes closer.
I tell my hands and they don't answer.

Berries hang thick on the fences
of the last summer I can remember.
I am trying for the sweet,
the sound of fruit.

There is a growth in me.
They will never find it
in time.

Gretel Now

This is the wood, but the witch is late.
Fruit drops to my hand and the nights are safe.
The trees are full of hide-and-seek brothers
grown thin as twigs in my easy weathers.
When I sleep I dream a threat
to push into the oven's throat.
I wake to a tickle of mice who ate
the careful road of signal bread.
How much longer can I wait
with the secret house inside my head?

Borrowed sweets are turning sour.
My eyes go old and murderous and yellow.

Inside the Blonde House

In the house made of snow-light,
books deaden between white banks.
Tracks of animals are filling up.
My feet see through floors,
this cold holding me.

Colors of pictures and rugs have gone out
like candles under a glass.
I may dig among kitchen drifts
with my paper hands, searching
for the strawberries in the story.
I could break up the furniture,
burn it.

I could eat my companions
one by one
by one.

Hall Mirror

Half ruined with age, it held
my clear child's face halved
by a botched future, impossible
dim old woman.

Now in the same glass
that child's eye is the dark one,
her mouth desperate as the bad half
of the witch's apple. Clearly the other
smiles, an eye of laughter.
The old woman knows what she's doing.

Everything changes sides.

Elizabeth, Cornered

Out of this
who can dance?
The spinster aunt knits my brow.
I remember the churchwindow
shedding saints' color like flaking paint.
I remember the grass face of my mother,
the stone she wore.

Once I dropped a live egg in the hen-roost,
watched the chick-sack's muffled beat.
I remember the fear of kisses, a shape
that still grows on ceilings.

Expose a pathos of breast and thigh
to the horned light?
to turn toad is better,
sitting a long time with rusty skin.

I saw a man who was made of birds.
He flew, a little at a time.
O the winged finger, the light elbow,
the lifted belly.

In the splayed house under my ribs,
I sit large and still as a portrait.
Who'd have thought the world thrown at me
out of God's angry fit could so have missed?

Skill

It is a dream I have often:
    I'm skating a pond to its risky center.
    Your eyes are there
    as if caught in a mirror.
    I skate the shape of your face.
    Either you will rise warm out of ice-shards
    (I have carved you a smile)
    or I will go down to you
    where the drowned keep old summers.

I wake to no choice, a cold sweat,
remembering that I haven't been taught
such surfaces, nor how to wear, moving,
a knife's two edges.

Looking for the Uninvited

You didn't come because you weren't called.
Not even a whistle in the dark
or a slippery accident
reached you. It can't
be said even that you wait.

Unhanded, in the only perfect freedom,
you are forever the day after.
What shape would you have given to this day,
a ripe plum, an hourful of grass?
Even the dead can do that.

What shape would you have taken,
you with the millions of possible noses?
Nothing can own what you own,
no one, jack of all minds in my trade,
unlived son.

Oversong

The words have come and gone,
those heavy footfalls.
This is a roomful of echoes, visible
as a web of cracks in the air.

Imagine the shattering of crystal
without original
sound.

In the net of this love,
in the wind, I am
a dark careful chiming.

Limit

We have done what we can
for each other:
one abrupt flesh broken
like light upon another.

Air

What we had was no more
than the space between us,
rich as the one clearing
to which the deer return.

When we lost it, the darkness
was too heavy to breathe.
We were two hands clapped
desperate as prayer.
When you pulled away,
the flesh of my hand went with you.

Now this hand grows a new country,
roads that don't want to arrive anywhere.
Across burnt distance we look at each other
like the two hands of one who never dreams.

Someday Someone Will Tell You This

Driving any night road as if it were the right one,
I wrap the country of this grief around me;
it is a plain shawl the color
of absences and rain.
Everything that has been erased remains,
though I move with two lights, though I move
and the hours scatter ahead like wet animals,
taking their small teeth elsewhere.

Things Left Standing

That summer I trailed the creek
every day daring to come
to the end of what I knew
with thin August water beside me,
the sun on the fields almost audible.

The last day, I turned with the creek
where a pine grove I had never seen
held a ruined country school, gutted
not by fire but by children
grown tall and permitted
their will among the unused.

In a coat of shadow and dead paint,
the walls seemed to fade, leaving outlines,
leaving one intact pane of glass
where the sun struck and gathered a shape
like the tow head of a child,
one who was left or whose ghost stayed
to study the seasons of corn.

Drawn in through a doorway of splinters,
I touched broken desks, touched
the smell of wasps, housedust, pine needles.
The back wall was gone,
the room left open and legible.
Names were cut deep in three walls,
and shapes: every sexual part, all things
male and female carved outsized,
whole new animals
in a wooden impossible book.

In the movement of shadow, that place
trembled with ritual, with the finding
that always is personless.

I spoke to the fields
severed names, fragments, forbidden
words notched crookedly, correct.

I lay down near a tree, slept,
and my dream shaped a man,
made simply of summer and grass,
who would take on a face, who would hold me
speaking the tongue of the touched.
I woke with the grass on my dress,
sharp stain that would stay.
The ghost that clouds any window
only at one angle of vision
was gone when I turned for home.

That which is given once
or thrown like a curse or a weapon
came both ways in the ruins of August.
I knew the dead child in the glass,
knew the sun with its open knife
and I stood up in the smell of the future
to wear as time had given
the green, deep scars of the light.

The Giver

for Don

Today I would bring you the rain,
sound of wooden gates you have forgotten.
I would bring you my hands full of letters,
the snail's track dreaming on the sleep of stone.
I want you to have the forest I lost
though its animals cry in my skin.
I would give you my one dawn in the Andes,
moment of light leaping the slow peaks.

I give you the child who weeps for us
naked in the dark beneath mountains—
the rain one drop at a time.

After Love

*from the custom among certain
American Indian tribes of
returning the bones of eaten fish
to the river from which they
were taken*

From pursuit we are bent
toward sacrifice:
fishing these rivers,
one takes on debts.

In the moment of leaping, we remember.
The deep dream will rise
in the moving smoke of our fires.

Now is a handful of bones,
kept whole in the shape of each life,
given back to singular waters.

It is barely enough, this
white song for afterward:
we ask the careful and intricate
blessing
last.

II

Southbound

Southbound

You can go back in a clap of blue metal
tracked by stewardesses with drinks and virginal masks.
These will work whether you breathe or not. And this
is the first part. The way is farther
into thin roads that sway with the country.
Through the shine of a rented car the red towns rise
and crumble, leaving faces stuck to you like dust.
Following the farms, houses the color of old women,
you gather a cargo from yards full of lapsed
appliances, tin cans, crockery, snapped wheels,
weedy, bottomless chairs. These float through the air
to rest on the sleek hood, the clean seats.
Things broken out of their forms
move to you, their owner, their own.
You slow under weight. The windshield blurs
with the wingbeat of chickens. The hound's
voice takes over your horn.
A green glass vase from a grave in a field
comes flowerless to your hand, holds a smell
of struck matches, of summer on rust, of running
water, of rabbits, of home.

Then the one place flung up like a barrier,
the place where you stop, the last
courthouse and gathering of garrulous stores.
You have brought the town.
It walks in your skin like a visitor.
Here, under the wooden tongue of the church,
by the paths with their toothed gates,
in the light of the drunk as he burns
past hunkered children reaching
for the eyes of their fathers, these fading
and coming like seasons,
you are the tall rooms of your dead.

Merchants still ring small furious bells
and the window of the moviehouse opens,
and the girls who will, open.
Men still stand jack-knifed to trace
deer trails in the dirt.
And blacks scythe the lawns, not singing,
keeping their flag hidden.

You may house again these weathers worn thin
as coins that won't spend, worn smooth
as the years between two who are old
and not fooled any longer. You may stand
beneath the cafe's blue sign where it steps
on the face like a fly. You may bend
to finger the cracked sidewalk,
the shape of stilled lightning, every fork
the same as it was when you thought that map
led to the rim of the world.

You may listen for thunder.

His Gift

My father loved my mother when she died.
After that he stayed away from houses.
He lived with the running of the hounds and foxes
who made an old fierce grief articulate.

I learn still from small animals of wood
he carved and put into my hands instead of words.

The Ceremony

We are smashing the clay pots.
Having come to last things, we
built up the fire. We
have reasons.

Shards in the fire are arguing
with spears of light.
Glue in old cracks has melted:
the broken pieces are like feathers,
standing black shafts barbed with flame.
Later the bones will stand
praying without color.

We have taken the earthfleshed,
taken the squat grandmothers from their windowsills.
Sculptural lovers and children and the angular
animals are gone, their hollows emptied of darkness.

Everything is jagged gates.

It is rumored that we will hear something,
a needle of sound like the rabbit's one syllable
escaped alone. We are waiting
in this light. We are taking notes.

Louisiana Line

The wooden scent of wagons,
the sweat of animals—these places
keep everything—breath of the cotton gin,
black damp floors of the ice house.
Shadows the color of a mirror's back
break across faces. The luck
is always bad. This light is brittle,
old pale hair kept in a letter.
The wheeze of porch swings and lopped gates
seeps from new mortar.

Wind from an ax that struck wood
a hundred years ago
lifts the thin flags of the town.

Ridge

The last pines
a stand of old women

Beneath their feet the plow blade
rusts and the bones of the mule move
through the eye of the lost
farmwife's needle

The Sixth Day

Here where the river is naming itself
in heat that clings like a history,
two men walk with their knowledge of snakes,
the dance of the hunter, though their step
is arthritic now, altered.
One is my father. He has come
to fish with his oldest companion.
And this is not the place, but near it,
near the thick woods, net of beasts
these men have lived in as one might
stay on in a treacherous house
because it is home.

They will sit out an afternoon's sweat
to salt the river with stories
of guns with second sight, hounds
with the gift of speech,
deaths that struck back.

It is like the way they run fingers
over the sharp dust of antlers and boars' jaws
and the head of a wildcat my father
has nailed in his barn.
They talk and the thickets tangle
around them. Their compasses
break. They come again upon phosphorus
in the deadwood of midnight, brighter than foxes.

The two men have drawn up a few fish.
The day runs them down, a dragonfly
dimming on water. They rise
for their homes in that light.
And the red wolf is not here
nor the bear nor the wildcat
whose head on the wall is not magic enough
to raise the dead.

The two men are leaving
without eyes in the backs of their lives
to see what I imagine: two images
left on the riverbank, two figures of clay
with rough, thumbed-on faces,
and not gleaming, not holy
but dark with the absence of pity,
an absolute love without knowledge.

I have guessed for my father an innocence
pale as water. He moves through it,
away from me to stride in his sleep
the deep land empty of animals, empty
except for the quick coil of memory
under the foot of his life:
the sure, small dream that kills,
that keeps.

Any Kind of Mountainside

The way out of this rushes past me,
fog's body I am to pass through.
Wherever I go I will leave
dark holes, mist torn to sculpture.

Later when pieces of darkness,
landslides in my likeness,
roll down heavy as history,
I won't believe their speeches.

Poem from November

The leaves have fallen, releasing the distances.
This year of my turning moves
in an arc like a preying bird's,
purposeful.

My loves have dried. I find
I can remember only the least things:
mouse-gray of my grandmother's hair
dead in the silverbacked brush,
the smell of hardpacked dirt
under black grease in the smokehouse.

Here is the old sky, the one we always had.
Everything in it is small,
punctuation for a vanished story.

I have forgotten the trick
an old man taught me: how the voice
can be made to nest in the cupped hands,
calling. Was it the dove
or the owl I brought close then?
There was a calling.
Something came.

Catatonic

The city is dreaming of the one street
of a small town, of houses with grass laps.
Deeper, an Indian village turns like Troy,
arrows floating to the surface.
Farther than wells go, animals are
whole in the skins of their deaths.
The earliest sea still lurches,
giving up roots and teeth.

The city dreams as far as it can.
We wake eye to eye, openings.
We make for the exits, rising
to emergencies like lovers,
the blood caught hard in the body,
breath in the throat.
And we go down again like water.

Visit to a Small Mountain

The shapes of balsam and laurel
sing like the quiet of old men
gathered alone.

Tickless water seeps in the rock's dream.
In air without seam or wound, even my footstep
keeps its own meaning.

Life stands up all over the body like fine hair.

Winter Place

On a slope with hemlocks
distance can be touched like moss
We drift
into the blind eyes of snowclouds
Between the child's two hands
air opens
Between his foot and the earth
a flower of strangeness

Somewhere a nun walks in snow
her dark habit gathering white
the feathery speech of a lover
on his way to becoming water

Directions for the Journey

The bird in the veins climbs
with song for the airless places.
Even the eyes in their closets
are opening blue gifts.
Now there are points of light like snow
so close they melt. Your hands
are flooding their maps with salt.

Island

It is dark here. I can say only
that I have never seen you, never.
Each day the sea places offerings
beside my footprints.
It is quiet here.
It will be quieter.

The sound inside seashells
is one gift that never unfolds.
The life coils hard around itself.

There are songs in the ears
of sleeping children
whose dreams are silence,
whose days will not return.

Coming

As it was before stairs of the vertebrae
invented themselves, as before wingbones
and teeth, as it was before
webs and singing came into the world,
something is not here.

Something is not here,
the new skin or the shining substance,
a bone in another place, a bendable word:
something workable as dreams
that do their jobs night after night.

I must bring it myself—
    one body to work with and not even
    a thousand years to fool around in—
there is no one else.

This is in answer to your inquiry:
already I notice a shadow.
Soon it will tell me its shape,
the terms of the new death.

III

&⁊&⁊&⁊ *Walking Out*

Walking Out

Fishing alone in a frail boat
he leaned too far, lost hold,
was turned out of the caulked world.
Seventy years he had lived without learning
how surfaces keep the swimmer up.

In that green fall, the churn of fear
slowing to pavane,
one breath held precious and broken,
he counted oar-strokes backward:
shore was not far.
This coin he took from the pocket of terror.

Starting over, over his head,
he reached for the earth.
As creatures of water once called on the future
locked in their bodies, he called on his past.
He walked. Walked. And there was enough
time, just enough, and luck.
Touching greenfingered sand, rising and touching,
body bursting with useless knowledge,
he came at the world from its other direction
and came to his place in air.

Back in his life now, he measures
distances one breath long,
talks less, flexes
the oars of his legs.

> Things shimmer where he is,
> his house, his earthcolored wife and sons.
> Every place raises walls around him
> the color of old glass.
> Heaven is a high clear skin.

Beneath the drift of flesh his bones remember
trying for bottom.

For Sylvia, Eight Years Old

In a wrung season, she hears the twig
touching its cold elbow, the wing
opening south, the water hiding
in the deep hands of the ice.

She answers the small doors:
worm, snail, the beetle prisoner
on his upended curve.

There, there the moth unfolds.
There the air parts for a feather.
She knows the wind's turn in the dust
and the steps of the rain.

For her the squirrel arches, and the bird
completes his invisible tower. For her
the cocoon's pulse keeps, and the web
stands in its two anchors.

Cornered in her eyes, the bright world
trembles unspilled, and that love
like the wind in her long hair
is long enough.

Sister, That Man Don't Have the
Sting of a Horsefly

> "However, woman can never be a
> poet. She is a muse or she is
> nothing."
>
> ROBERT GRAVES

But doubling's a speciality among us.
She looks from my mirror, that other's
face nobody suspects me of.

Part of the light in my eyes,
blind Texas sun I grew under, color
of brass, her face is loud as a street band
and as flat. I know how it feels
standing behind the "Eat-Here" counter in the bus station
still as flypaper, waiting for the next one.
She's that kind of weather, never
taking no and never going far,
lighting up one after another.

The bastards don't bother her
wanting that brassy light she's got,
wishing she'd get out of theirs or at least
take one of them home before she marries a plumber.
Years she's been mopping up
after babies and truck drivers.
Nothing they say surprises her.

After the Visit

Friend of so many years,
(at fifteen we wept together because Jesus
wasn't a thing to believe in anymore and because
we were afraid of sex and death and Latin)
it was good to see you again.
How is it that I am thriving, too plump
on nothing a month and very nearly
the same old fearful questions?
You are so sad, so thin,
nervously smoking in a rich house,
having seen the world and found Zen.

Fantasy at a Poetry Reading

Tonight the bear is given his weight in meaning.
An elk wears flowers in his antlers. He'd eat them
if he could reach them.
The wolf is received as a brother. No one asks
if he'd rather be an only child.
A few Indians have been arranged for,
solemn as caterers.

Suddenly some unworded animal
steps live out of shreds of poems
and the room fills with the scent
of the utterly separate.
Poets fold inward like struck tents.
The creature (an otter? a badger?)
walks across them,
leaving like Roethke's meadow mouse
for the best possible reasons. Leaving
delicate prints no one can read.

At the Fair

Before even the glorious ferris wheel,
we wanted the animals. "Wild!
Exotic!" yelled the menagerie man.
Inside, we watched the molting hawk ignore
for the third year in a row,
boys and their sticks. The fox
caressed his cage door with a furious muzzle.
He was new, unused to noise.
We counted splinters in his nose.
The giant bat uncloaked himself, a mouse-mouthed yawn
and wing-tips touching wire on either side.
One old wildcat stalked his shadow
while his eyes stood still.
When we had seen them all,
we moved to the music and wheeling lights
where people were passing each other.
Behind each fixed look something quick walked,
jerked at the end of its chain, turned
to cross a face again.

News Items:
"Ex-Star Lash LaRue Arrested as Vagrant"

I rode the heaving theater seat
to the last crack of the good whip.
You put us all in shirts with silver buttons.
Badmen dissolved with the jail key's absolute click.

Now it turns on you.
Years with the carny circuit roll,
coil around you in your cell.
On the damaged screen inside your head
the outlines of your face go bad.

I'd send you a clever cakeful
of myths and money, only I wait like you
in a small room which seems to be locked.
The lights are on. The last scene
flaps in a machine that won't stop turning.

Watching My Daughter
Practicing Gymnastics

Headstanding, overriding,
you hold any edge of air and dive
into motion that waits for you like water.
As you turned in the dark room of my body
you turn in this room of light.

Sure of a grip and any angle,
your tall form denies everything:
my years, gravity, the furniture,
all crimes you won't accept.
Like the walls your motion moves,
my flesh blurs, heavy and unable.
I am turned with time after time, dizzy
and breakable, breakable.

The Return

for Garland Adcock

The family names have waited
like teeth inside the stone lip of the wall.
Nearby the barn that is falling
is telling its rosary of nails.
In wind and freezing rain a brothy light
holds us. The hole in the farm
holds us at edges.

He ran from this ground. It lived on
in his face, all mute and desperate cycles.
Every year a crop lay down and died,
a winter came that could not be got over.
Now we sidestep hummocks of ice.

Wind shreds the silly prayers.
A single bird cry drifts, breaks off.
The abandoned bends to him:
earth in his ears, the one right word for grief,
the curse he would himself have spoken.
We freeze and cannot weep.

Pastime

They are barely themselves
Deer and bear and coyote
Whittled from pineblocks
By a man who liked hunting

He leaves them unfinished he leaves
The dust furring their backs

He is old he dreams deep completions
Sharp eye and hoof-edge
Tine and claw in their sockets
Himself tall with weapons

Mornings his spine aches like a tooth
His foot slips climbing the small hill
Eyes fail at pages he loses
Names and time

Things come to a finish
detail by detail

Again Then

I have come and I watch
you stroll your dusty townful
of ancestors and upstarts.
You carry a blindman's cane,
the mutter of old age.

The family name was the rattle in my teeth,
money you hoped you had.
The family lands leached like a grave.

I used to try to keep the leaves alive
after they had drifted to the porch:
I was that sure of light.

Words tapped my way here:
I use my own stick,
and I have learned to meet you, father,
dark to dark.

Vegetarian

I step inside their circle,
boundaries of beanrows, my friends
with their gestures of cornstalks.
I sit at their green tables
where salt stains the plain fare
in spite of us, bad water
at the cabbage root.
Even the seeds smell of cold sweat.
Brown children are crying in the rice kernels.
Afraid of what we are, we try
for the innocence of straw.
Burst huts in Asia scatter
a throw of bones, fire-gnawed.
We are sleeping for another dream,
hoping to wake toothless,
wise.

Answering the Psychoanalyst

The long-legged living goes on
in thatched rooftops beneath this time,
in our sleep where the house is always
early and part of the earth.

Stork wings in updrafts of the blood,
red legs meadowing in the sun of our darkness,
from deep migrations they bring their legends,
language of blows.

And we wear stories woven in rooftrees
the way our faces wear firelight, the way
our eyes wear blue chill at dawn.

Nests of strong thorns are gathered
to rock ghosts, those white eggs,
the luck.

Word-Game

A child watching a moonrise
might play a game of saying,
might hold the word moon in his mouth
and push it out over and over.

To make a sound like a fruit
repeat itself in the tongue's tree
is to forget what you know.
The word will grow, will cease
to be saying, will turn by itself
into tears into flesh into burning.

What rides in the sky will be free
of any name that the earth has heard
as though someone had severed a string.

In a net of sound like the body's
own singing web, a child
will be rising
with light for a language.

IV

❧ ❧ ❧ *Water*

Water

She lay on the ground with one hand thrust out palm down across the shadow's boundary. She could almost count the shafts of sunlight blunting their points on the back of her hand, the grassblades under her palm. These would pierce the flesh if she lay here long enough.

The paint on the house behind her was old. If one rubbed a finger against it, the stuff came off like chalk on the skin. The house shed its gray-white dust onto the green lawn. Perhaps that falling outlined the shape of the house, lost in the depths of grass. If there had been a lake, certainly a likeness of the house would have floated on its dark surface. If there were a lake, there would be a breeze to ruffle the grass and the hair of her arms.

She thought about the absence of a lake. Round, probably, or oval with little irregularities. But that was not the case. The absence of a lake was a blot with no edges.

The absence of a breeze was force without movement. She lay almost asleep in the heat behind her lids. When her eyes opened, the sky came at her like a sound she could not hear, widening blue circles.

There were no clouds. There would be no puddle of rain beside the porch such as she had once dipped into with a pin on a string when she was a child. She had hooked floating oak leaves which fleshed into fish as she pulled them up. That was the game.

Feeling the sting of the light, she tried to move her hand. She was pulling something out of the hot grass, out of the puddle, out of the fine gray paintdust. She could not see what held to the hook at the end of her hand. She pressed curled fingers against her cheeks.

It was the breeze from the lake which made life perfect after all. It drove the hot sterility from the house the way a broom drives dust before it. And the lake with its dock and little boat filled in the spaces in the days. To look from the road was lovely, to see the white, white house with the lake shining beside it in the slant of afternoon. The eye of the lake was never lidded.

If she moved close and put her face down, she could see the thread-like segments of movement which striders and tiny snakes left for a moment on the water's skin. At night the grasses spoke with the liquid voices of creatures living at edges.

And there were fish which could be caught from the boat, fish which seemed to be shafts of the water itself, shocked into solidity and broken off.

When she was younger, she had gone away. She had taken the house and the lake with her like one of those magical toys too real to play with. She had gone away. And it had seemed that she was following a thread laid by guiding hands, a little silver thread which wound its way into schools and cities, into offices and shops, braiding itself into the sad old names of rivers.

If there were a lake, she would cool her hands in it now. She would watch the droplets separate and come together again on her wrists. She would leave the grass pressed down in the shape of her body and her outflung arm.

Pausing on the porch steps, she looked at her place under the tree. There was no pressed-down outline, no shape at all. But the little silver thread ran from the shady spot to herself.

Always now she would find it behind her as if it had its origin in her body. If she looked around suddenly, she would see it trailing after her, attached to objects she had touched, staying. Sometimes, coming into a room, she would imagine a tangled skein crisscrossing the air, barely visible, like the motes of dust one can just make out in a sunshaft.

Making her dinner, she watched the sunset from the broad window by the dining table. Tomorrow she would take a picnic. She would go in the boat and bare her shoulders. The colors ran from the sky onto water where they spread and grew restive.

The windows were open. They were old and stubborn. She had struggled with them because there might be a little wind. Perhaps there was a thin movement, but it was warm and slow. If there had been a lake, the wind would have cooled itself on the water and quickened.

When she could hear the croaking of frogs over the sound of her radio, she stood up. To lock the doors? To open them? Something caught her foot and she fell, tripped.

Now the silvery strands were clearly visible. No longer thin, they had a ropy texture. She could see exactly the number of times she had touched the vase, the sewing box, the corner chair. There were so many. The strands gathered around her lightly, lightly, as though they had always held her and she hadn't seen what caused the gentle pressure, might even now forget to notice. But she could not move all the same.

If passersby should see the skein on the lake, or the boat, on the grass, they would only mistake it for a bit of web shining with night dew.

She lay still and silver under slats of moonlight, under the news from the radio tangled with static.

She woke in the dark and threw off the sheet. If there were a lake, she would get up now and swim naked as she had done once in another place. The air in her bedroom was warm and full of dust. It pushed her back into sleep where she saw herself seeing a lake and clapping her hands, wondering why no one had put a house beside the water set so perfectly among the trees. There was a small cleared space in her dream, as though someone had thought of a house and been interrupted.

When she woke with sun on her face, her body felt strangely hurt as if the muscles had been tightly pulled. She would not think of it. She would take her breakfast to the dock where the water would shine and speak.

Carrying her breakfast tray, she stepped onto the porch and closed her eyes. Something would happen. In the dark she had made, she worried the object in her hands the way the mind catches at memory, trying to place a scene.

High above the porch September's oak leaves began gently their letting go.